WHEN EVENING COMES

DOUGLAS J. CARROLL

authorHOUSE®

AuthorHouse™
1663 Liberty Drive
Bloomington, IN 47403
www.authorhouse.com
Phone: 1 (800) 839-8640

Published by AuthorHouse 07/14/2016

ISBN: 978-1-5246-1714-1 (sc)
ISBN: 978-1-5246-1712-7 (hc)
ISBN: 978-1-5246-1713-4 (e)

Library of Congress Control Number: 2016910882

Print information available on the last page.

ACKNOWLEDGEMENTS

*I want to acknowledge Mary, Carol, Donna, and Kyleigh (observer),
helpers, critics, friends, and companions in this journey of faith.*

DEDICATION

This is dedicated to my Aunt Ruth, a woman of curiosity and joy.

Author's Note

*When Evening Comes began as a daily observation to a friend who was
sick Every Evening I sat down at the computer with the hope of
gathering up the day just past with thoughts of affirmation for a quick
recovery. It always ends with an expression of Love.*

*I will from time to time use words in unconventional ways there will be
times when I omit words intentionally other times missing words are an
error It's your call*
*Words are not crafted but shared from the me part of me. Like gathering
pebbles along a beach gathered from the givenness of a day*

*Each day is a rare gift given without condition some are rough and edgy
others smooth*

January 24, 2011

The day past has been one of beauty bright
sun clear sky. The prospect is for another
two dog Night.

May the love and affection
        of heaven be with me.

To lead me and to cherish me
        this night.

Lord may your Holiness surround my
bed and bless my home this night.

January 25, 2011

The day past has been a quiet one Cold but
not bitter. Bright but still grey. evening is fully
here. We look toward the night to come.

Hide us under the shadow of the shadow of
your wing Keep us as an apple of your eye.
With that as the promise we can relax.

Find renewal in this night have confidence
that we will be held and nurtured. A new day
of Beauty and promise will emerge.

Good night Know that you are Loved.

Doug

January 26, 2011

All in All a still day but not a blank
one temps above freezing I think
could catch a hint of things to come.
Mud Time

Be Still and Know. The simple beauty
of grey against white and umber lines
drawn to define the grace of it. Indeed
be still and Know and be Known.

What a setup for the day to come moving
through finding Peace and a Holy Rest.
I lay my head down Lord confident.......

Be Loved and Love one another

Doug

JANUARY 27, 2011

Morning brought Grandma Moses
snow in the air, mid-morning bright
sun clear sky, Early afternoon a Heavy
blast of snow. Today a sidestep.

A day to pause put aside the busyness
You know an old sweater day. I recall
as a child sleeping in my father's car.
Nothing more comforting than his sweater
and the aroma to find him in.

Could it be that we need to be more in
touch with all that an old sweater is.
Take an old sweater into the coming
Day.

Have a peaceful night,

Doug

January 28, 2011

Snow started last night has persisted
and continues. Our Road is quiet and
the woods are still. Perhaps an early
night call.

I so often find that the best thing I can
do is just be still. To take time to listen
to the silence and have it speak. For a
lack of a better way to say it. Let the
silence speak.

Thank you for listening. Let us take our
rest. The silence will speak.

What comfort there is in knowing we are
Loved.

Doug

January 29, 2011

What a day!! A day of quiet wonder.
gentle snow that has changes the
texture of the land scape.

A day that sneaks up on you. Watch
all day and never see the change.
It's only after we look away and
look back with a new view that the
change is obvious. My journey in
faith has been a good deal like that.
I call it the Aha.

A tear comes as I Ponder the unceasing
renewal. Yes we can take our rest
knowing the coming day will be new.

May we be bound together in Love and its
Beauty.

Doug.

January 30, 2011

A midwinter day full of trickery. The
Bright sky clear of clouds and full of
Sun fools me into thinking it might be
warmer well not bad till wind chimes in
with my mother's voice button your coat son.
Where's Phil when yeh need him?

That's what mothers are all about comb your hair
do you have your license? Don't be out too late.
Perhaps there's something of the Divine woven
into those admonitions that can't heard at the time.
What Love and Grace it must take to be a Mother.

Clear sky midwinter = Cold night. Let's join together
Let's listen for those expressions of Love Love that passes
understanding. May God's grace be in us.

My love to you! do you have your.....................?
Smile rest well

Doug

January 31, 2011

A shaft of rainbow like light came down
above ending at the tree line where it
met the sun rising marking a new day.
Is it possible for a sunrise to be soft and
gentle? and yet have a core of brightness
making a statement. Did I hear it saying
I'm here let's get on with it?

My life has been marked by let's get on with it
events. I guess you could call them Redemptive
But that's quite a mouth full for me. No I think
let's get on with Sunrise. That just suits. I have
always been one who needs to keep it simple. So
I don't get all full of it. So if we lose our way
look for a Let's get on with it Sunrise.

Let's gather up a new day assured that each has
in it the raw material to create a
                 Let's get on with Sunrise
Thanks for sharing your time with this seeker of Sunrises.
With Love let us seek together

Doug

FEBRUARY 1, 2011

All in all today would have to be called a Lurking
day. With all the weather soothsayers promising
snow and ice from hither to yon. Do you have your
provisions in? Milk bread peanut butter what more
would one need? And the day still lurks.

Well that's just the way some days are without any
clear direction. I guess we just have to be alert
not to get caught up in the lurking or figuring it out.
Days are more precious than that. It's the givenness
of each day that we celebrate there is Beauty to be
uncovered oh it's there. If the big one comes perhaps
it's saying be still celebrate the silence. If we can't go
accept that gift Listen to the silence with heart.

So there you have it the day just passing and the promise
of a new day. Be confident of Love given without condition.
I will soon seek sleep Wrap us this night in the beauty of
Holiness.

With love one and all,

Doug

February 2, 2011 Groundhog Day

This is Punxsutawney Phil's day. Quite
a prediction only 6 more weeks of winter.
That shared with Candlemas time to bless
the farm equipment and to look to spring.
Half way there it's all downhill to spring.
Today was a this or that day it just didn't
seem to want to move one way or the other.

All of the above reminds me of how it is in
this part of Eden. I call it stone kickin' time. It's
the time spent in the barnyard sizin' one another
up. For the new kid on the block it's getting
accepted. A hot August day it was I had dug a
hole looking for the wellhead. Lyle pulled in his
pickup said Hi and we talked a half hour or so Me
in the hole tossing stones Lyle in the truck with AC.
I was covered with a slurry of mud made of dirt and
sweat. As he left he called down to me. "If it's
the well you're lookin' for it taint there it's over there"
as he pointed about three feet away. Down the
drive he went.

A this or that day. Oh Lord support us all the day
long until the shadows lengthen and the
evening comes, and the evening comes. Amen
Amen

With peace and Love,

Doug

FEBRUARY 3, 2011

Sunshine from start to finish. Cold
but not bitter. The early harbingers
of spring declare that they are
confident of a fruitful future. Let's
go with them. Let's listen to the tempo
of creation.

I have come to believe that the rhythm
of creation is found in the sounds and
sights and smells of each new day. Thank
you for this day, thank you for this night,
thank you for the sights and sounds telling
of your presence. Thank you for your Love.

As we seek our rest this night help us to know
you in a Holy quiet. As a new day emerges
from the darkness may we find our rhythm
in the sounds and visions and the aroma.
Grant us to share its wonder.

May we go to our rest in peace in thanksgiving
for the grace and Love

Doug

February 4, 2011

Close to bitter cold this morning with the wind.
Our Let it snow flag that hangs by the
kitchen door was doing a great dance.
How's that hokey pokey go and then you
shake it all about. I think I may have
seen a snow snake or two. Even with
sun the cold persisted.

Sun snow and it reminds me of Snow Angels.
And thus the Angels that have come by during my
journey. None have had wings or trumpets.
They have come in all sizes and shapes. It was a tough
Angel Who gave me a job that allowed me to go
back to College. The day I came to start work
he called me into his office, He said "I don't need
to hire you but if you want to go to school you have
a job. And if you quit school your fired." There's
another side to tough Angel Charlie. Perhaps another
time. Angels you see do all sorts of things they announce
they challenge they patiently stand by and they listen.

As I go to bed this night I will lay down and make an
angel. And find comfort in knowing I'm not alone. May
the love of God gather us up.

May we have peace secure in His Love.

Doug.

DOUGLAS J. CARROLL

February 5, 2011

What's to be made of today? Got
off to a beautiful start enough sun
to say so. High clouds to the East
in rows like sheep. All in all a drifter.

I find from time to time the Me part
lets a drifter day set the pace. As I
took note of this gift of a day. A sculptor
has been at work removing a bit here
and a tad there removing the sharp
edges. Creating a new landscape.
BEHOLD I MAKE ALL THINGS NEW
Beauty emerges before our eyes without
our seeing.

As I seek rest this night. Perhaps as I
open my self the sculptor will change
my vision to see more clearly the
garments of God.

I find comfort in the Love we are so
freely given. Amen Amen

Doug

FEBRUARY 6, 2011

Another start with sun though this
day it warmed flirting with above
freezing. It had that look in its eye.
Perhaps the romance of Mud time.

Start getting things around the hose
too frozen to the ground to recover
from being out all winter. Too dark in
the barn the shop lights don't work too
cold. Well at least I got some fresh air I
rationalize. Must be a message in it. I
know it's Phil up to his old tricks. Sure
it's Phil all right.

I smiled as I closed the Barn door and
turned seeking safe harbor in the house
tea perhaps. We'll claim it as a planning
Day and be thankful that the real Senior
Observer has a sense of humor listen
yes I hear it too letting us have our folly
and still Loving us.

As I seek my rest I will smile gather up that
special pillow thankful so thankful.

May his Love be upon us all.

Doug.

FEBRUARY 7, 2011

A quiet day never far from anything
a mid winter day can bring. The tug
of war has been won the prospect
of rain has been fulfilled.

Today one of learning some by choice
most by chance. My life has been marked
by days like this. Days I call turning stones in
a stream to see what's there. Splashing
along turning a stone here turning a stone
there. A life of discovery and learning.
That's me a turner of stones.

How often it has been that I've been given
stones to turn. Could it be grace? I'll have
to keep an eye out perhaps something else
turns the stones?

Find peace this night let another hand turn
the stones. WOW that's cool.

Bound in the love of the Lord. Let us find
Rest My brothers and sisters

Doug.

FEBRUARY 8, 2011

The entire valley was washed with
a sun filled sunset to the West more
saturated to the East the clouds
gathered the colors softened them
turned them inside gentle, violet
and peach with others whose
names cannot be spelled. Enjoy!

Others whose names cannot be spelled.
What a gem of a day! A gem that refracted
the Sun and a hand that cast it West
and East. We find in this day that might
have otherwise been cast aside is one
of redemption in a brief sunset.

A gem of the everyday hidden in a brief
sunset. As we seek our rest give thanks
for not having missed it. In Peace wrapped
in Beauty may we take our rest.

May our homes be the place where Peace
wrapped in Beauty resides. With Love

Doug.

FEBRUARY 9, 2011

Morning came without note light pushed
the grey back while evening just put the
lights out without even a hint of sunset.
Morning gathered the Sun, cleared
the clouds bright Sun through it all.

Clear days COLD nights with the wind
bitter. Long johns time to check 'urn out
make sure the flap is shut tight it might
be time for Duct tape. How can we go
wrong a gem given rough cut accepted
What with Phil leading the way and
Duct tape to fix it move into it all with joy and
fearless abandon.

Fearless abandon marks the pace and
purpose of the journey. Beauty on every
side, hand in hand with Phil we are joyous
and fearless.

with the Love that binds us together.

Doug

FEBRUARY 10, 2011

The sun barged in bright and bold
all of a sudden a new day! Brash
and Cold the fact of the sun did not
help the thermometer much. cold and
bright ice crystals and a light show
blue red gold they twinkled in the air.
A smack down day.

So there you have it Bright Sun Bitter
cold Brash Beauty do something with
it. Kick back and celebrate it all clear
cold beautiful. Enjoy the wonder of this
day. We tend to carry a negative view
from the start. put that aside find the
wonder of a creation made new

Let us rejoice and be glad. Alleluia
Alleluia.

Seek rest this night Alleluia, Give thanks
this night Alleluia. Rejoice and Alleluia
Alleluia Alleluia

Love,

Doug

February 11, 2011

-8 degrees with no promise it
would get much better. A gradual
slide as the day advanced toward
evening. Let's just rejoice and be
glad in it.

It's Friday and I got to thinking how
sad the number of days I missed by
looking forward to Friday coming.
Sad it is that I have spent so much time
looking forward to this or that allowing
the gift in each day to pass unnoticed.
After all it's a day we are given with all its
secrets, and beauty and wonder. Perhaps
staying in each day with its smells and
tastes and sounds and sights is what it's
about.

Let's scoop up this day be thankful in it
and for it. And the busy world is hushed
and the fever of life is over and our work
is done ....

In the Love of the Lord,

Doug

FEBRUARY 12, 2011

The day started and ended with
muted grey and snow heavy at
times. at noon high winds blowing
and snowing snow white out no
visibility and poor visibility. you're
crazy to be out in this.

Days intrude and say do this
because only you can and it's the
right thing the loving thing to do.
That's it being there just being there.
I ponder, "how often have I missed
just being there." a white out a black out
I can do better than that.

May our homes be a haven of blessing
May love cross the threshold and be
welcome here and our just being there
be an expression of love.

Love one and all

Doug

February 13, 2011

A little bit of this a little bit of that.
Sunrise and sunset about the same.
The day did a soft shoe routine.
May be it was a maybe day.

The woods chatter and clatter these
days, beginning to feel their oats with
impending spring. They must listen to the
early sounds the Juncos the white-throated
sparrow and hear and feel the presence
of the Pileated. Let's take this maybe
day to listen Be still and know and
perhaps to learn.

Not a bad day all in all. As we go to our
rest may we find ourselves in tune with
the rhythm of the quiet sounds.

with Love,

Doug

FEBRUARY 14, 2011

The morning had its paint box out
coloring the horizon using orange
red yellow and magic colors. Full
sun a warm breeze that carried the
aroma of spring. By noon back to
reality -8 tonight.

Days can be like that our hopes of
a promise morning get caught up
by reality. Let's not get ahead of
ourselves The gift of each day has
everything we need. gather gold from
sunrise a gem from the aroma of spring.
hammer the gold with the energy of
afternoon fashion a ring for our finger set
with a gem. WoW a gift like that not bad
not bad at all.

May we seek our rest this night
May we be safe in our homes
May we be wrapped with a blanket
of Love and find refreshment.

With Love,

Doug

February 15, 2011

Started cold ended cold I say a fickle day
almost a step back you'd think those
of us from here would be ready for
these days but we never are. Surprised
again by the obvious.

There we go again getting ahead of ourselves.
is it wanting something and trying to push the
day ahead. Trying to put a square peg in a
round hole. How many times I've done just
that. over and over look at the hammer
change hammers. You get the point.
put down the hammer and peg.
It's called acceptance of both self and the
day. let it be let it be

I seek rest this night May the Holy of Holies
enter my home may the Holy of Holies
be my companion Holy Holy Holy Lord
God of Hosts

With Love

Doug

FEBRUARY 16, 2011

Bright sun ushered in morning dragging
it over the horizon say good morning now
what is there that you don't understand
about GOOD MORNING. SMILE you're
Loved even in the morning

Thank God for that. I'll bet you figured
it out I got up later than is advisable.
I seem never to catch up to the day
it's always a step ahead, I'm always looking
at the bottom of the shoes of the day out
front. The watch word for today is STOP
There is no catchup! acknowledge that it's
gone. Start over pull up what ever it is that
you pull up and get about the business
of celebrating every day fully. There are
gems to be found and polished and given.

Soon it will be time to go to my rest. may I
find refreshment As I close my eyes may
I leave the door of my heart ajar so that
which is Holy may come in

Love,

Doug

FEBRUARY 17, 2011

There it was a hot orange peach orb
slapped above the horizon. Morning
up to her old tricks sneaking around
below the horizon and jumping out
and pasting that sun in the sky to
make morning. gotcha!!!!

Days can be like that. They grab
you no lingering today saying move
it out we've got Lions to beard and
dragons to slay things to do people to see
and the day kept changing what it
had to offer just to keep you off
balance it has all stopped now a still
calm now the day is over night is
drawing nigh shadows of the
evening How well I know those
words Sung by my mother during
Evening Prayer. The voice of a
simple faith.

May I this night seek rest with a
simple confidence in the Love in
the Love and with thanksgiving.
Amen Amen indeed now the day
is over.......................

With Love

Doug.

FEBRUARY 18, 2011

This was the day of the Promise of
Spring. To start with it had it all Sun
the Aroma one of those days you can
almost Taste Warm breeze. a Promise
so heavy wore down the day so a late
afternoon take back. Be confident Mud
time is upon us.

Mud time the time when you can hear
the tap tap tap on the bottom of newly
hung buckets. It's all about Mud and
magic and lost sleep In the midst of
fire and steam and a bubbling cauldron
the elixir of Spring is conjured. Some
times days are like that out of fire and
steam and mud comes the reward of
a golden sweetness. A golden sweetness
at the end that brings us back, Life
indeed a golden sweetness give
thanks in it Let it be
Mud   Fire   Steam

And the dog still needs to be cleaned up
before you seek your rest May we find our
rest this night confident of His love and
and hand in the making of the Sweetness.

With thanksgiving with Love

Doug

February 19, 2011

It started out with that look in its
eye. That kind of wink that sez
something's up. The high Winds
continued through the night always
a portent of something. at noon the
jig was up. Winds Snow both from
the sky and just blowing in all the
wrong directions. no question a
full Hunker down day.

you just know a full hunker down day
You know these kind of days
when they come. The Wagon master
yells circle the wagons we'll ride this
one out. Thank God for days like this!!
Gather all the hunker you can find it's
some times under the dog cauz dogs
are masters at hunkering. Got your
hunker in a pile? Now jump in (no one
ever got hurt jumping into hunker)
Ready? now just listen don't think
don't plan just listen. Listen to what?
ready this is the Biggie listen to the
silence. listen to the silence. listen

Bless my home with Holy silence
Bless your home with Holy silence
Wrap us with a Holy silence

with Love,

Doug

February 20, 2011

What a Day What a Day. Cloudless
sky rare over this part of Eden. The
Sun brilliant without heat. I've come
to the conclusion that the back side
of the Sun has a hidden, and never
revealed till this very moment, heat
sucker. and the sucker and the
heater duke it out and the heat sucker
wins now and then. Enough of science.

a day given a day received a push pull
givenness, On this kind of day the hard
part is being the middleman. To and fro
to and fro. once we find our balance
and listen for the music, are there any
days without music? and its rhythm.
We are safe to go with music and
rhythm and the motion. Can you hear
it? faintly to start. we are one in the
spirit we are one in the grasp the rhythm
the motion Rejoice and have fun in it Damn
the prediction full fun ahead. laugh be
foolish laugh and be glad in it do you see
over in the corner yes I believe it's the Big
guy tears in his eyes laughing till his sides
hurt.

Lord as we go to our rest may the rhythm
of this day be the very rhythm of creation.
the laughter of the day define us.

with joy and side wrenching laughter

LOVE !!
Doug

February 21, 2011

heavy snow to start a reverse of yesterday
that started with full sun as the day moved
it tried to mend its ways by noon the snow
tapered off to nothing try as it might it just
slid along and slid on till evening saved
the day with darkness. 7 degrees tonight.

an easy day to lose to just let slide by.
But this day had another start a Quiet one
Look beyond the falling snow Look at the
new landscape Behold I make all things
new That's it there before our eyes the
Snow sculptor reshaping and covering
I see in it the wonder and raw Beauty
a scene so close and to think I'm part
of it. I have been invited into the very
studio of the Snow sculptor not as a
visitor but as a participant I almost let
the snow define the day the evergreens
adorned in Ermine as though a master
tailor with scissors in hand a mouth full of
pins snipping here and there stepping
back Perfect. I believe we are all invited
in to the studio of Snow sculptor into the
shop of the tailor. It's our choice to accept
the invitation.

Thank you for this day thank you for the
vision thank you for the invitation each day
offers The Sculptor and the tailor have laid
down their tools may we lay down any
heaviness and find our Rest and find our Rest.

with Love
Doug

FEBRUARY 22, 2011

Day pretty much ended as it started
The Sun strutted a bit mid-day to little
effect.?????? Cold will press in this
night 1 degree if it stays that warm
just checked my secret source looks
like -3 spit snapper

Life gets going some times and before
we know it our direction is circular like
a top. And what do tops do? become
a blur. So let's take a Red up day it's
a day to just stop spinning. In the shop
sweep sawdust enjoy the aroma of
the various projects. put tools away
a finders day. by golly there it is. Be
thankful for just stopping and for the
newness. amazing what a good
Red up will do.

We can seek our rest this night with
thanks in how just stopping renews
refreshes heals. may rest be sweet
for you

With Love

Doug

FEBRUARY 23, 2011

Today has been a slider both figuratively
and literally. a layer of melted mud on top
of a layer of ice now that's slippery. Perhaps
this is it the first step toward Mud Time. a
true harbinger of Spring.

There I go again getting ahead of myself.
Perhaps I interpret What I see to suit
myself. That's the problem with wanting
something a lot your vision gets out of
whack Time to take stock make sure
that what you think you see is what you
see. let's wait till we see buckets hanging.
then we will know it's MUD TIME

Let's be thankful for having been brought
to this evening let's be peaceful with
ourselves it's a place to start with joy
and thanksgiving. Our MUD TIME will
come in due course indeed indeed Let
us find our Rest

with Love,

Doug

February 24, 2011

A day that could have just passed
by without notice. I tended to think
it stayed the same all day, But the
signs were different and by mid
afternoon the puddles under foot
said thaw.

I sometimes lock myself in a box
That's the way it started that's the
way it is. As one who calls himself
Senior Observer I fall down on the job.
I need to tune myself to the day to
feel what's going on many times a
good sniff tells the story don't drift
off into the maze of assumptions
take a gentile grip and let the day
come to you. Oh the beauty of
discovery.

May the beauty of discovery grant
us a night of revelations. as we seek
our rest may we be at peace as we
open ourselves to the beauty of
of discovery

may your rest refresh

with Love

Doug

February 25, 2011

Morning came in with a vengeance
Heavy blinding blowing snow no
visibility stepping back another sight
all of the windows were white as
though they were an artist canvas
gessoed ready for that first bold stroke

find the pallet stand before the easel
make that first stroke. Sometimes days
are like that they call upon us to look
inside. into those hidden places perhaps
never before touched. Don't pass up this
chance for newness reach in gather up
what's there spread it on the pallet make
that first Bold stroke of discovery. WoW
and to think a snow storm a snow.........

a day a gift of discovery I seek my rest this
evening thankful that I took that second look
we can rest secure that a chance for discovery
will come with the new day

With Love for sharing this evening

Doug

February 26, 2011

We found them just up the
road just as the light was leaving
without event. Ballerinas! nope!
12 or 14 of them Senior High girls all
decked out in their prom formals
some standing stiff for fear the top
would not stay put innocent and
Beautiful every one.With better light
there would have been a blush.

I'm thankful for that image and for
the day that offered it what power
there is in these tiny vignettes cast
about for us to discover.

May peace be with us this night
may we be still as we seek our
rest. may the night be gentle

May Love hold us

Doug

February 27, 2011

All in All I would call it a mousey
day you know that color a day sitting
still waiting to do something or perhaps
nothing. on the cusps of mud time?

between us the day is full of signs. Can
you keep a secret? (the sap is running)
smile to yourself puff up your chest yep
Mud Time is here. go ahead be a little
Smug you can even strut your stuff.
This kind of secret makes a day Hawks pileated
woodpecker skunks. mousey day yep
go out take a good long sniff fill your
lungs there you go taking on spring.
For celebrating Good Hot Mug of Tea
Scones or better still Oatmeal cookies
with raisins.

Let's seek sleep this night with a smile
that we didn't let a mousey day get our
Goat we out foxed it good for us.

With my warmest Love,

Doug

FEBRUARY, LAST, 2011

Let's just call it Hump day we have
been pushed over the Hump like a
rail Road car and there is no going
back. Another Mousey day started
with rain ended with a wink at Sun.

Not too bad a day to usher in MUD
Time. Let's just poke fun for that's
what Mud season is. Just think of
it if you dump buckets sticky shoe-
laces hands jacket pants. then Fire
boiling sap DON'T BURN THE PANS
Steam swirls nothing seems to
happen the night drags on steam
and fire has its own magnetism
people out of nowhere no matter
what! mud is the order of the night.
Stories told about women and life
sometimes death the steam swirls
with urgency and the magic the liquid
too turns gold Now look at the dog
why is that dogs love to run the
ruts.

Be calm let us seek our rest with
a smile. May we find peace this
night. It's ok to poke fun at a day
for it's in the fun that Love is freed
to find us.

with Love

Doug

MARCH 1, 2011

The Sun had to struggle to shake
off the low clouds once freed a Bright
day throughout This time of year the
Sun's not accustomed to staying out
all day to be seen by evening it just fell
beyond the hillside.

the usually quiet stream speaks of
heavy snow melt. the sound like the
Rush of a train going we will know
when its safe when the stream falls
silent. I am finally still after a day that
sums as lots of try and little achieve.
You know a computer day.

I will soon seek my rest and I must say
I look forward to pushing the sleep key.
I have looked forward this day to this
chance to chat. Take your rest in quiet

how beautiful it is I end each day with an
expression of Love to each of you

Doug

MARCH 2, 2011

Slept in Sun didn't it was up crashing
around. The Sun just getting over the
hill had to jettison all the heat.by mid
morning a white out The Wind came up
the woods complained about no heat to
no avail The sun gave a late shot of
color as it limped then fell out of sight

It has been a day to gather up and
smooth off the rough edges then hold
it up and to say softly it's a bonnie
one. yes rejoice and be glad in it.
Redemption was always found on
this kind of day as the trees clattered
outside the knitting needles did the
same inside there would be tea; and
a cookie or two from the tin under
her chair. That's redemption gathering
a day smoothing off the edges seeing
that it's bonnie and letting the knitting
needles make it so.

I can now go to my rest at peace even
in the telling renewal comes yes it's been
a bonnie day. Good night

Love,

Doug

MARCH 3, 2011

Morning arrived without event Sun
in evidence above the widely scattered
flock of sheep. Traveling through this day
was like walking down a high vaulted corridor
the farther along we went the more muted the
day became. No sunset to speak of.

March indeed in like a Lion. As a kid I could
never quite put that together. This day has
had sharp edges. Wind gusting on this cold
sunny cloudy windy calm Contrasts perhaps
that's what the Lion Lamb thing is all about
Big ole blustery Lion gentle sheep. A true
transition season we look forward to what
it ushers in gentleness love. The sweet
aroma fresh beginnings.

We may seek our rest the lambs are there
waiting in the wings. I'm thankful for your
sharing these days and what each one has
for us. fluff up the pillow(s) snore if you want
this is a two extra huggggs night

Love

Doug

MARCH 4, 2011

The sky over this corner of Eden has
all day reminded me of old home movies
Flicker Flicker Flicker man this is great
I think that was uncle George or was it
the dog?

I have days like that Just keeping the film
moving if you don't instant smoke sometimes
fire. and there goes uncle George's priceless
film of the Moose Hunt. Yep there are days like
this you're so busy keeping the flicker going
nothing much else is accomplished. Don't get
all worked up. There's something to be learned
here. It has to do what I call Folly the film is
flickering we will never know if it was uncle
George or the dog.

We come to our rest knowing a wee bit more
about ourselves Rejoice. Give Thanks for
this day

Love

Doug

MARCH 5, 2011

This has been a sameness day from
start to finish. Every time I was out
it was the same. No telling what
time from one time to the next

Days like this are Gems in the rough
These are days that say stay alert
I'm reminded of the prayer "Keep watch
dear Lord for those who work or watch
or weep and give Your Angels charge
over those who sleep." that's watchfulness
Have confidence there is someone watching
the store.

We can seek our rest with calm yes indeed
be still and know. I'm thankful for this day

Love,

Doug

MARCH 6, 2011

Started with snow ended with snow
for me I'd look out and think it was
about to stop it didn't still hasn't

a friend called to report that the
sculptor was out and well and working
in his back yard on looking out he's
here too. could there be more? simple
tools only a pallet knife. gotta say he's
good! Fine snow not the best material
for his chosen tool. What do you think?
a demo with a message? yeah that's it a
demo with a message.. That has to be
what it is a demo with a message. Simple
tools simple snow

Enriched we are every day by the simple
those happenings that change our vision
change our heart change our very being
snow a simple tool a demo a message
May we each seek our Rest with simple
faith.

Love

Doug

MARCH 7, 2011

No bragging rights for either end
of the day the middle part
Bright Sun few clouds though cold
a keeper.

I have never before in all my born
days had a hound dog sing Happy
Birthday to me. My first experience
with Hound Dogs singing was with
my father coon hunting Fall nights
with a snap in the air They would
sing the chase and the treeing The
music of the forest brings floods of
memories the best apples I've ever
eaten each dog with a voice of its
own marking the chase and its end.

I have never had any one sing Happy
Birthday to me with more sincerity than
my hound dog friend. The vibrato was
great. I can seek my rest knowing I'm
Loved.

Love

Doug

MARCH 8, 2011

bright day good sun but cold.
Late this afternoon the Coyotes
announced their presence, wonder
if they have a den near by?

There are seasons like this where
a pattern sets up and seems to go
on forever. we set ourselves up to
see each day as same ole same ole
rather than taking each day as a
separate gift offered for our joy and
enrichment. The splendor of creation
cast before us to touch and smell and
hear. We live each day in the midst of
a restless renewal let's let this day
turn us inside out and make us a
New creation.

As we seek our rest let the restlessness
be like a cradle rocked by an unseen foot
rocking to the cadence of creation.

Love

Doug

March 9, 2011

This day came in like a Lion and
strutted out the same all blustery
mark it down as a good blow.

no doubt the day was blown in
for us to catch It was as though the
chicks at the farm store were blown
in every direction as the young father
tried to catch one for his daughter to
touch. What a joy!! for the child? yes
The true joy and excitement was mine.
One of my spring rituals is to see the
chicks in the farm store. the bonus
watching young parents young children
touching the very essence of life
preserve for them that wonder
with Creation.

I'm thankful for this day and for the
gift of a moment to gather up and put
in my pocket. think of it the wonder and
beauty of creation in the farm store.
I go to my Rest content join me.

Love,

Doug

MARCH 10, 2011

From a nondescript start misty
grey we puddled through until
the heavy rain washed the day
out of sight.

A day the Observer has enjoyed
full of hints marking a day of
promise Geese heard but not
seen the red maple has taken on
its purple head dress as its buds
swell even on a rainy day the sugar
maple casts its red glow that
escapes the camera. Skunks
announce their presence both by
sight and scent. The stream is up
and the last remnants of snow will
soon be gone. For the Observer not
a bad day for gathering hints. Not at all
bad not at all bad.

The hints abound but we can take our
rest now not a bad harvest for a day.
May our rest be shrouded in peace.

Love

Doug,

MARCH 11, 2011

The sun got up shook itself off and
held the overcast at bay till Noon Then
the sun packed it in as the breeze
sharpened its edges and lowered the
temp. By evening snow.

One of those days it's easy to lose.
The flag laying flat like a magic carpet.
What a ride it would be over the big field
down by the stream. The stream sliding
by played a light show early with the sun
sparkling off its troubled surface sneaky
it minds watching.not much more to over
filled. Days can be like this a little bit of
this and a little bit of that all of a sudden
too full. Help us to keep watch Lord these
slickery days can knock us down. Indeed
Keep watch.

It's time to seek our rest. The kind of rest
that's given offered at the end of the
day for our peace and refreshment.

Love,

Doug

MARCH 12, 2011

Today just about everything Sun
Rain Snow Bright Sky and to think
we lost an hour of it overnight.

A day to smile about to gather up
and be thankful for. These simple
gifts we receive and so readily take
for granted. Each day like this is
another step in the journey plain
and fancy rain or shine each marks
our journey days come in all sizes
and shapes it's not for us to pick
and choose. Our task is to celebrate
it the best we can. It's on the off days
that we discover why we are not alone
you know the days when we need a
hand up so often by someone we
don't know and may never see again.

Go in Peace to Love and be Loved
We are connected bound together
It's safe to seek our rest in the
knowledge we are not alone
Thank you Lord for those hands up

With Love

Doug

March 13, 2011

Blustery cold snowy slippery
little sun lots of grey Shorter
to say March day. At least not
a step back

Words are wonderful creatures
they so often have a mind and
will of their own they must be
nurtured and sometimes given
their own head, at least for me.
Only when I let words speak to
me can they speak for me. Its
been a day like that for me when
Words lurking here and there
not always wanting to be clear
for me. Photography is better
gather an image compose let
the image speak for itself the
language does its own thing.

The image will emerge if we
step back and let it tell its story.
You see the story is us and in
it we will find and be found. I
come to my rest at peace. Thank
you for talking with me.

With Love

Doug

MARCH 14, 2011

A quiet day flags hung down the
wind Chimes were silent bright
but not enough sun to cast shadows
on the remnants of snow waiting
for spring

I write tonight with a sense of stillness
an inner quiet not often given this
restless spirit. it's striking that the inner
spirit is stilled on the day of quiet. Perhaps
there are more still days that just get
blocked out and the space filled with
stuff. It's on the still days that a freshness
flows in to carry us no need for us to
HELP dare to be still and to be renewed.
The restless side resists let it go let it
go. I will go to my rest this night aware
of the givenness of those times of stillness

I go to my rest thankful for this day
Perhaps you have found some stillness
in this day to take into the night

Be Still and Know With Love

Doug

March 15, 2011

The bold start to the day was
not to last as the sun chose hide
as it warmed the stillness also
was sacrificed. a bit of this a bit
of that March at its best

This time of year can con you
into believing that things are not
as they are. That a different set
of rules are in effect. I recall as a
kid the first idea if your team got
behind was to change the rules.
Our wishes get all piled ahead of
reality and for all that clutter things
get out of whack. Just open the
front and back door on a March
day reality sets in fast clears your
head and frees your funny bone to
rattle and get you snickering and
laughing The wonder medicine of
laughter will set things straight.
Laughter is like a Bowl of oatmeal
it warms your soul and sticks to
your Ribs. Thanks Mom!!

Let's seek our rest with a broad smile
The kind of smile you can put your
arms around. What a wonderful
day.

With Love

Doug

MARCH 16, 2011

A bright grey day the sun lacked
the courage to get out in the open.
even without the absent sun the day
had a gradual warming. over all a
nice late winter day. After Sunday
a nice early Spring day.

Throw in an equinox and suddenly
two days change their names late
winter becomes early spring. Days
just don't get no respect. After all a
day is a foot print to mark our progress
on this fantastic journey. There are
other ways to measure progress but
the day is the perfect size and shape
to get hold of. I have never had a day
that didn't manage to expand to get
us over a hard spot or shrink to fill in
around the edges. That's what it's all
about providing the raw material so
the day can fashion foot prints Our
job is to put in the best we have the
day will take care of the rest.

There has been a softness about
today gather up a bit here a bit there
and seek our rest.

With Love,

Doug

St. Patrick

The day started with promise to
be fulfilled as the day marched
ahead WoW A day a day to hug
Then a Sunset that spoke for it
self and then some. A WINNER

Today was a collector one you
wish you could keep and have
for another day. a foot print you
want to remember. Beauty promise
fulfillment and a rich blend of
contentment gather as one to
to create a tapestry marking
the way. A fleeting edge of
color leading us into evening.
No looking back this evening
only a moving forward with
hope. I'm thankful for this day
for the richness and promise
A WINNER you bet Lets take
our winnings

With the Winnings under our
pillow and a sigh of contentment
on our breath let us seek our
rest renewed and anticipating
the coming day.

With a warm Love,

Doug

March 18, 2011

An assertive Spring day a warm
one from start to finish. We are off
to a great start.

She's tired tonight long trip in the
car new friends not being able to
decide inside or out. so many new
choices what will it be this or that
in or out the air filled with the incense
of spring. Is it any wonder that spring
is the season of wandering off of those
chance meetings and conversations
with the skunk and the assertive
outcome. a whole new day of wonder and
beauty filled with promise the richness
of new she and I can share it together
The two us checking the fit of the
jacket of Spring. What a wonderful
gift those first few days of Spring
finding ourselves stunned by it.
Thank you Lord for the gift of this day
and a friend to share it with.

We can seek our rest this night
content in its wonder thankful for its
beauty. this night will bring rest the
morning a new wonder

with Love

Doug

MARCH 19, 2011

The sun slid over the horizon undercover
The cloud cover waited and provided
cover as the sun slipped back over the
horizon. And Evening Came.

There are days given from time to time
to share and renew. Renewal is necessary
time that's so often put to the side. There's
always tomorrow it can wait. Truth is there's
only today. Capture the Beauty of days like
this they will make your heart sing. Rejoice
in it. On a journey there are from time to
time places to pull over to enjoy a scenic
view time to stretch our legs to walk a bit
and to just plain see. It's ok to step out of
the fast lane and enjoy the moment.
The aroma of Coffee this morning even
before the sun had decided to get up
A moment of beauty a time to put in
your pocket next to your heart that's what
makes the heart Sing.

Rejoice Rejoice just a day to be. I will seek
my rest this night in peace Let us be still

With Love

Doug

MARCH 20, 2011 EQUINOX

Vernal Equinox Hard to believe such
an otherwise plain vanilla day can fill
those big words. Spring now that's
better.

Spring suits me better first day of
Spring that's one I can feel it has
all the aroma of newness it has
motion and texture it's a day of wonder
beauty. Every once in a while we
have one of these little gems given
to us a day to accept and let be.
It's hard to accept the little gems
without trying to figure them out. you see
these are not days of the head but
rather days of the heart. indeed days
that make your heart sing.

We can seek our rest this night with
a song in our heart and our soul filled
with the Beauty of Holiness. Amen Amen

With Love

Doug

MARCH 21, 2011

I find it hard to describe this day
grey its full length it ended with
the full promise of rain. Let's call
this one Mishmash.

My day pretty much followed that
theme. I think today just carried me
along for the ride. I had a friend in her
90s Who described learning to drive
as a young woman and that her father
told her to just keep 'er between
ditches. And she had driven that way
ever since. You know there are days
that just keep 'er between the ditches
is the best we can do. These are days to
take in stride steer a course that keeps
us out of trouble. These days are learnin'
days days that teach you that you don't
have to be in control. I'll take this keep
'er between the ditches.

Keep 'er between the ditches I now seek
my rest in comfort. Kick back relax smile
be aware you are Loved

Love with peace

Doug

MARCH 22, 2011

The vault of the sky today reminded
me of silver hammered to a uniform
sheen and a glow. Muted only by the
rain. Reflective

unlike yesterday today was one to
just take in. A day allowed to speak
in its own quiet voice. I sometimes
miss this kind of day because I tend
to fill all the space with my stuff and
block out the wonder provided in this
solitude. I know that I would benefit
from more solitude and less stuff. It's
stuff that blocks the hearing and feeling
of the heart. more often than not quiet
leads to those places where we are
made whole. May God grant us that
completion found in Solitude Amen
Amen Amen

May God sustain us as we seek our
rest. May the quiet of this night hold
us safe in the comfort of solitude
Amen Amen Amen

With Love

Doug

MARCH 23, 2011

Snow heavy overnight had by
morning Festooned the forest
with all manner of doodads that
only snow can produce. Instant
Wonderland.

snow this time of year has the
potential for turning everyone
into a Grouch. After all it's March
23. Spring unlike any other
season is the time for everything
Spring is evasive on the move
Spring is a dance with a rhythm
all its own It's a time we are on
the look out for but never capture.
we can hum the tune feel the rhythm
smell the newness yet never capture
Spring is most often the season to
look back on it's never a time we
can gather up and put in our pocket
It's the most anticipated and the
most often missed. let's just live it
love it and let it make us smile.
Be thankful this day and all like
it

I go to my rest this night thinking
the master artist has done it again.
Rejoice and be glad in it A snow
angel or two. it's said My peace
I bring to you My peace I give to
to you

With Love
Doug

MARCH 24, 2011

Don't quite know what to make
of today sunny but not warm a day
without features grey calm
cool sunny Like a pile of play
dough in need of a hand.

That's it a day that needs a hand
a hand to be there a hand you
can count on. a hand up a pat on
the back a hot cup of tea a cold
drink a hand to wipe your brow
to catch a tear, to tie a shoe lace
there's something of the divine,
the hand of a child a baker a
mechanic. sure looks like the
divine has snuck up on us. to
plant a seed to nurture creation
Come Holy Spirit Come

May Holy rest be given may Holy
Rest be received. May the hand
Holy be with us this night

With Love

Doug

March 25, 2011

The sun thinking she was hiding
behind the snow got all worked up
and turned the horizon a delicate
peach perhaps a promise for the
day ahead?

A promise that just hung there and
slowly slipped into grey. The snow
went from Grandma Moses to heavy
bright grey following. You have to love
it how we get all worked up not having
it the way we want. This day is a gift
a rare gift Full of light and life and
wonder if we would just let it happen
let's try being joyous at having the
day let's throw in a bit of thanksgiving
that we have been here to live it.
Find someone to Hug, if there's no
someone Hug the dog. you get the
Drill stop moping start Hugggging.

Let's seek our rest this night with a
heart filled with joy and wonder find
the old pillow count sheep when the
bed fills with sheep sleep will come.
be at peace you know it's even ok
to be silly!!!!!!

my love to you and with you

Doug

MARCH 26, 2011

Alleluia! Alleluia Let's just Shout
and acknowledge this ordinary
day for the gift that it is. What
kind of day was it? Special.

It's so easy for me to get it
backwards. Let's start with
Alleluia. The day is not lacking
the Alleluia it's there every time
If we don't see it it's not the day
that's lacking it's our lack of vision
the Alleluia is always there.
Why's that so hard? The Alleluia
makes a request then we put it
on out where it can be seen
Alleluia Spread it around in
abundance like peanut butter on
warm toast. Let the Alleluias begin
and end each day

As we seek our rest gather a
spare Alleluia or two and pray
them for someone who needs
one. once we start giving Alleluias
they never run out the more you
pull from your pocket the more
there are. Alleluia Alleluia Alleluia

They never run out
With Love

Doug

March 27, 2011

A rare cloudless day bright
mid 20's A day that warms
your heart. Pretty.

There are days like this one
where stillness is in order
The givenness of this day
spoke from the edge of
Eternity I spoke of Journey
and of Alleluia A friend a
journey shared and ended
and begun with only an Alleluia
separating them

I seek my rest this evening
with stillness and with the echo
of Alleluia to the ages of ages.

With Love that fills those softest
places Alleluia

Doug

MARCH 28, 2011

The Sun made it over the horizon
first thing and stayed till evening
making its exit with night's advent

A feel good day For me the
crispness of the air blended with
the radiance of the cloudless sky
Hawks were active along with a few
Canada Geese and fewer Buzzards.
All good recommendations for flying.
The wonder of creation enforced by
those ordinary activities of daily
comings and goings. It's in the
everyday that the divine is to be set
before us take it in and live it out.

I seek my rest this night secure with
an awareness of the divine's nurture.

With Love

Doug

March 29, 2011

A bright day ok under foot
for getting out a camera
snow a dirt road woods
images. DIVINE

Some years ago I picked up
a camera after a long separation
I was not then nor now prepared
for the new vision both out there
and inside. It indeed makes my
heart Sing. Wonders and Friends
Blessings Discovery of self. This
evening I reflect on a span of time
as DISCOVERY for which I am
thankful.

Stay by this night Lord stay close
this night Lord in the everyday
where I live it's in the every day
that I find you and am made new.

To each of you Love

Doug

MARCH 30, 2011

a gentle day light breeze Sun
to spare Looks like March will
go out like a lamb

Each day as it is given to us
is a blank slate for us to write
another bit that tells our story
Some days slate filling is easy
and the images fit in place with
ease others take more effort.
so be thankful gather up the
bits and pieces if they don't fit
today set them aside one day
they will

I look forward to this night content
to leave pieces on the side one
day they will fit May a Holy rest
be upon us

With Love

Doug

MARCH 31, 2011

More bits and pieces of winter
to gather. Perhaps the Lion
won't leave without one last
Roar.

Light snow overnight covered
the car as morning warmed the
snow slid across the windshield
and gathered in folds reminding
me of a fair linen gathered by
altar guild in anticipation of vesting
the Altar for Celebration! Each meal
has the potential for Celebration
They are the intersection of the
divine and the ordinary. let's
welcome holiness it takes only
providing a place.

I look for rest this night with a sense
of the nearness of things holy grant
each a holy rest a peaceful night

With Love

Doug

APRIL 1, 2011

Neither end of the day made
itself known. even the part
in between was not notable.

Days like this come about from
time to time For me a day not
without achievement but
without much texture smooth
a day that just slid by. Perhaps
it will be a marker day and set a
new pace and direction a moving
toward Easter with Its promise
of finding a new way

I seek rest this night with hope
expectation and joy. may the Lord's
love be in you now and always

With Love

Doug

APRIL 2, 2011

As the last of the snow recedes
the newly visible tells a story of
secret winter activity evidenced
by daffodils above the ground.

As I share a day with you I'm aware
that each of you has a day unique
A gem of its own making The journey
as well although sharing parts in common
is single it's for us to live in and through.
Some days are like opening a gift. What
wonder each has. the daffodils? Perhaps
spring has been doing its own thing!

The breeze of this afternoon has stilled
Lord grant us each a night of holy stillness
an inner calm and a peaceful rest

With love

Doug

APRIL 3, 2011

A day full but not crowded sweet
but not overly so. a day of quiet
enrichment smile.

Days like this speak out of the
quiet. they gather you up and
quietly hold you making you
whole in stillness. the realization
that quiet and stillness are rich
with the energy of creation thus
this quiet day speaks and makes
us new

Go before us Lord into the quiet
grant that we may find our rest
there where you are.

Love

Doug

April 4, 2011

Thunder made a valiant attempt at
waking the sun without success
added blasts of snow and hail no better
result. Grey from thunder to night.

Each day is given to us in its best
outfit. We too should dress a few
hugs a smile on our heart. we
don't know what's ahead perhaps
a box of tissues day a shoulder
Look for Beauty offer Joy be
prepared to laugh. make a final
check gather together the
assumptions put them in the
closet. hum a tune say gotcha.
Be thankful !

Let's seek our rest with gratitude
and may we find in this night rest
and a path for the coming wonder

Love

Doug

April 5, 2011

Woke up to Grandma Moses snow
more gobs than flakes that drift
down and evaporate what magic
in the air. Good soooo Good

entering the cookie shop I was
greeted with "where have you
been" and a hug what's better than that?
Then we sat right there talked about
family the long imposed hibernation
cars and cookies, Some would say
small talk I'd say Big talk what's more
important than two people caring
to get caught up? The stuff of living
the essence of being as we talked
nothing else mattered time that had
no agenda I'll take that any day! Yeah
that's what it's all about cookies and
getting caught up not enough flour
on my jacket from the hug next time
you bet. It's these times where the
everyday divine speaks.

I think I can still smell the cookies
so I seek my rest at Peace may we
each find our rest complete

Love

Doug

APRIL 6, 2011

A day mostly still a combo of
Rain and Snow. Temp the
same till now Wet mouse
day.

Do you ever have what I call
an aha day a day when you
are given a solution to a problem
for me they most often go with
you dummy that's been there
all along. It takes my tripping
over the obvious to learn this
or that. To add to that the day
has mapped itself in such a
way that I can't check it out
till morning. now let's talk about
patience Who me well you get
the drift

Nights are given just as days
and I seek rest this night in
hopeful anticipation of the
sun rise.

Good Night with Love

Doug

April 7, 2011

The Sun missed a chance to show
Clouds triumphed again it's not that
I don't like clouds but this time of year
Sun helps a lot.

This day has been a gentle one.
a day given for us to make something
of. These are the sleepers they should
be raised up and turned into celebration
like is says on the stamps I bought today.
I buy stamps that will brighten my day
today I bagged two one a sheet of jazz
and a sheet of celebrate with fireworks.
Take this day Jazz it up and celebrate
with fireworks Look at that a plain ole
vanilla day has become a party, Some
days all it takes is a couple of stamps
and letting it all hang out I think I can hear
the trumpet and the sax Is it possible that
renewal and newness can begin right
there in the post office?

I'll bet the farm that it can I seek my rest
confident and sleep well Trumpets fireworks
Let the rhythm ease your soul into holy sleep.
the drone of the Sax setting the pace.

Love

Doug

APRIL 8, 2011

Off to an early start this morning
Me not the sun It stayed undercover
all day not even as much a how
do you do.

Another marker sign of spring
the first peepers Not the full
blown symphony it will be as the
water warms. It will be fits and starts
One night they will tune up the next
not a sound. The first full peeper
triumph song is when the dog
hears them. It must be that the
peepers and their incessant calling
wake up the other swamp livers.
That's where it all starts the swamp
Water that baptizes all things and
brings new life. We will soon begin
to check them in as surely as the
swamp warms new signs arrive.
Another day of wonder another day
to be thankful

may we have the grace to discover
in each simple image of spring the
renewal of life I will go to my rest as
I hope you will listening to the simple
voices that are Spring

Love

Doug

APRIL 9, 2011

Down right Hot between the doors
what with the Sun out finely doing
what Suns do.

I celebrate this day and evening
the aha learning of the other day
came to its full productive fruition
enriched perception it's like adding
understanding to vision. Each day
is journey held together by smaller
side trips to hither and yon. let's
take each day smile no laugh at
ourselves find the wonder in the little
things and the big will take care
of themselves

Lord be with us this night as we seek
our rest help us to hear your breathing
and feel your touch let us be still and
know

Love

Doug

April 10, 2011

This day has gone by with a wee bit
of everything the organizing cast
taking a bow. bits and pieces sun
breeze not cold damp not wet

The cast has asked me to extend
an invitation to the cotillion the great
dance of spring The migrating
cast is in place Robins Starlings
The little brown 'n' grey jobbers.
Hawks 'n' Eagles 'n Buzzards mark
the sky as they work on their routines
stirring the pot of creation Owls will
soon be fledging their young the dance
goes on. The fixed place actors rush
their tableau to completion setting buds
Rhubarb pushing through the soil and
placing its thumb sized rocket launchers
buds swollen on the forsythia the maple
will soon retire for this season The profusion
and the richness is too great to capture
The invitation to the cotillion is for you
to join the cast

I will seek my rest this night humbled
by the invitation to the cotillion of creation
to find renewal

With Love

Doug

APRIL 11, 2011

the day kicked off warm with
the feel of rain and the hint of
of a storm

The day was a stage setting
day all day the Avian choir was
quiet I suspect checking seating
and music scripting the dance.
Things of the soil had their day
One could almost feel the energy
of growth not hard to imagine given
the dashboard reporting 76 The
peeper chorus is fully gathered
the ebb and flow of their voices
fill the valley along with a fine rain.
I have heard that some have already
begun to fill dance cards,

Let's find our rest this night assured
all is well the cast is here and plans
are well underway.

With Love

Doug

APRIL 12, 2011

A hint of Sun a hint of Clouds
a hint of Rain a breeze with
an edge. Spring at its best

Everything coming on stage
is new and fresh and clean
What's left to do for myself
it's time to do those things
only I can do the self cleaning
soul polishing to get ready for
the dance. I know I need to keep
from having spring fever
close my eyes and ears. Take
the time now to order things
so that the upcoming celebration
will find me ready. we too are
to be newness and freshness
so evident In the freshness of
the voice of peepers and the
newness of the green of spring

I seek my rest this night asking
to be freshened Thankful for this
day and the night to come

Peace and Love

Doug

April 13, 2011

A quiet mousey grey day rain
or almost rain all day cool not
cold.

A day that could lull one into
falsely thinking that not much
is going on but it's a day full
of energy and life and growth
I know I need days like this
a day that takes you aside
and without much notice fills
you. it's as we come to make
the connections with the little
sometimes tiny bits of life around
us. Indeed as we gather up the
small bits and pieces that we
recognize our part in the cotillion
of creation. I have a friend that
remarked about the vineyard
that there's always something
going on where does it start?
right where you are now. The
dance has begun let us rejoice
and be glad in it and to think
a rainy day.

I find rainy nights good sleeping
nights and I seek my rest this night
knowing that there's always something
going on

Love

Doug

April 14, 2011

A day marked with birdsong
a day that felt like it was ready
to explode.

The cotillion of creation is well
underway The birds with their
urgent messages I know of a
man who went this day to visit
his granddaughter and his brand
new great granddaughter they sat
close together to have a talk about
the awesome wonder child birth
is, how's that for a dance in the
cotillion of creation. To share a
moment and move on. Life is I
believe the sharing of the bits
and pieces and making of them
an offering of the fullness of life.
Be open allow your dance card
to be filled and the Lord's grace
will fill you Thanks be to God.

I will seek my rest this night as
I listen to the music and feel its
rhythm

With Love

Doug

April 15, 2011

A breeze from start to finish
neither sunrise nor sunset
were notable

the descent was more a tumble
than a fall almost like a small
plane headed for a crash when
suddenly the large dark shape
righted itself and with purpose
rose almost straight up a very large
bird acting out a ritual only known
to him. a short observation and the
large dark shape raced down the
valley perhaps for another
performance I find myself energized
by all the movement and growth
Lord take us by the hand and guide
along the way Help us to find our
place renew us

let's find our rest and give thanks
for the gift of life lift our spirits as
we see the wonder in those little
bits like a falling bird the purpose
in its recovery

With glory and honor praise the
Lord with love

Doug

April 16, 2011

Rain driven by harsh cold
wind set the tone for the
day

Every season has its exceptions
days that pull us back to reality days
that say you're not in control They
say to me get your priorities straight
take a time out get things in order
it's that givenness of life so we take
a time out find our place find our
way and are touched by the divine
a divine presence that's always there
and needs only to be acknowledged
and celebrated

The rain and wind have stopped and
I seek my rest grant me rest this night
and a quiet spirit to be found by you

with Love

Doug

April 17, 2011

The day threatened to improve
all day and failed ending in a
mishmash.

We are given days from time
to time that are what I call
pointer days or perhaps stage
setter days. This day Palm Sunday
is one of those it sets the stage
for the week to come as we
ponder the events that led to
Jesus death. grant us grace to
hear with our heart as the story
is told so we may be enriched
to continue the journey with
thanksgiving

I seek my rest this night at peace
that this journey is one we share
I find both comfort and courage in
that

With Love

Doug

April 18, 2011

A day without much direction
The wind and the rain were
cold enough to be chilling
that way all day

Stations of the Cross at church
this evening to set the tone and
mark the direction of the journey
The journey that we each make
is not always easy. it requires us
to go hard places, for me the
journey is not singular but rather
a collage a gathering together of
many journeys bound together
by grace, and an abundance of
Love. People and place coming
together making the journey(s).

I seek my rest this night with
thanksgiving for this day May
each of us find our rest in peace

with Love

Doug

APRIL 19, 2011

The day grey rain wind now
still First spring Bear last night

we continue our observance of
this week we call Holy All n all
it's been a quiet day for me We
get the mistaken impression that
this journey is all motion yet I find
my journey has required stops to
gather things up to take stock
perhaps to find out where I am
and where I'm going. pulling over
onto one of those scenic overviews
to take a deep breath. If we're always
in motion our vision will be blurred.
Perhaps this week we call Holy
requires stopping and being
still and doing nothing. We don't
need to get anywhere. Just be still

I am thankful for this day and for a
chance to pause in this company of
faith. I seek my rest calm knowing
that the Lord's grace will hold me.

With Love,

Doug

April 20, 2011

A warm day sun sun and clouds
rain threatened to no avail not
bad not bad at all.

This week we call Holy continues
A stop day yesterday a day to be
opened We will now turn to gathering
the images Some of the images
are not easy by themselves much
less to put together side by side.
betrayal denial set with compassion
and love. A tableaux of life for us
to be and to ponder. continue
the journey and allow the vision to
unfold this story is for each of us
to become, to know

Seek rest with peace be covered
by the hand of the spirit. Sleep
well be refreshed

With love

Doug

APRIL 21, 2011

An uneventful day as the
tug of war goes on between
seasons.

our journey continues during
this week we call Holy. we
gather to break some bread
and share some wine and to
remember Jesus' act of humility
in washing the disciples' feet.
For myself I find that it's best
to open my heart and listen.

I will seek my rest this night
with an open heart seeking
a sense of quiet and stillness

Love

Doug

April 22, 2011

rain snow sleet not much
of any of it still too much
for most

The journey continues the
tableaux of the cross and
death is set before us not
so much for us to ponder
but rather for us to envision
having told the passion
story we eat what was left
of last night's supper and we
strip the altar removing
all signs of celebration
the church is darkened
the tomb is made ready.
We wait Open our hearts
and souls as we watch and
wait empty us as the journey
continues into the darkness
may we continue our vigil
in Hope

May we seek our rest this night
in watchful anticipation keep us
steadfast in the journey(s) Amen

With Love

Doug

APRIL 23, 2011

The day Beautiful just
Beautiful it warmed and
I'm sure lifted spirits

The Great Vigil of Easter
The Lighting of the Paschal Candle
The telling of the Story of deliverance
The journey of the people of Israel
The Story of Creation Genesis 1:1-2:2
Israel's deliverance at the Red Sea
Exodus 14:10--15:1
Salvation offered to all Isaiah 55: 1-11
The Gathering of God's people
Zephaniah 3: 12-20
the journey I speak of had its start back
there and goes on we are on this
journey together. we are individuals
and a corporate fellowship all at once.
The Journey is begun anew the candle
is lit the history is read new bread is
blessed and eaten new wine is blessed
and shared.
Alleluia. Christ is Risen
The Lord is risen indeed Alleluia
An empty Tomb speaks for it self

Let's seek our rest knowing that
we can never be alone and our
place on the journey is assured

With Love Alleluia Alleluia Alleluia

Doug

April 24, 2011

For as late as it is in April
I hoped for a warmer and
dryer day got neither.

Easter Sunday I have many
images Don't miss Church
day Easter In my family the
whole family gathered "Up
Home" that place my father
had moved from but never left
our extended family always had
an abundant supply of Easter egg
hunt children Uncle Roy would go
down the lane with the children
looking for the easter rabbit while
the men hid the eggs (I learned
years later) At the appointed time
on their way back Uncle Roy would
shout there goes the rabbit and the
hunt was on. The lawn once empty
was now covered with the color Easter
What better Easter Alleluia than the
excitement of those of discovery of
those children. Easter for me is about
discovery those children got it about
right. Alleluia Alleluia Alleluia

The candle is now lit anew to show
the way may it be our guide as we
seek our rest this Easter Evening
alleluia

Love
Doug

APRIL 25, 2011

A grey day still bits of rain

Easter with our newly found
farm family. On a time line but
not rushed. a full complement of
generations down to the new
born great granddaughter (to
some) a new member for all to
love great grandmothers danced
the who gets Baylie first dance a
full slate of subjects wet fields
ditch digging plowing planting
things that work and those that
don't. by midafternoon every one
leaves chores and milking to be
done. Farmers are people of Faith
and hope they take the day as
given and give back the abundance
of the harvest. They have in their
bones a sense of resurrection.
And so we prayed and we ate and
shared the givenness of this Easter
Sunday.
He is Risen He is Risen Indeed

Seek rest in peace my sisters and
brothers

With Love

Doug

APRIL 26, 2011

Sunny morning gradually
warming to afternoon rain
thunder lightning hail wild

There are days when it's
just as well to pack it in
go take a nap and turn off
the computer. This is one
of those

My your night be restful
With Love

Doug

APRIL 27, 2011

the day almost Hot it seems
that When Evening Comes
Thunder comes along with
a full complement of fireworks

The day has given the gem of
daffodils The colors this time
of year are unmatched Gold
and green of those spring
shades as we journey toward
another season so freely given
I so often take for granted a day
and let it slip by without notice
I have been one to look back and
forward while missing the now
yet it's the now where we live
you see it's in the now today
that we live its each day that we
are given to celebrate the fullness
and the givenness of each day.
Lets look and find resurrection
where we are

Each day is a gem to polish
may we go to our rest enriched

With Love

Doug

APRIL 28, 2011

A beautiful Spring day from
start to finish

Sometimes we are given a
day that calls upon all the
senses to take in fully on one
of those days one can smell
and taste a day that gathers
up the fullness of creation of
renewal birth the plow as it
turns a furrow the first step
in making a field fit for planting
that ritual act of spring looking
toward harvest. These days are
rich with hope. These days when
we all have a touch of good
fashioned Spring Fever take
it in let it happen We all share
the rhythm of creation. listen
to the peepers they have it right

We can seek our rest this night
wrapped in the fullness of creation

With Love

Doug

APRIL 29, 2011

Typical Spring day sun
clouds almost rain cooled
toward the end

I write tonight with thanks to
you as today completes 3
months of these bits and
pieces. I want to share my
thoughts about the way I sign
the bits of me with you. The
word Love has been degraded
over time and yet we are called
to Love one another as we are
Loved. It seems to me that Easter
is all about Love given as a gift to
each of us. I sign each of these
offerings with Love because that's
what's on my heart. I also want to
make visible that it's OK. I will share
more with you as time and space
permit.

fluff up the pillows tonight seek rest
celebrate this day

My Love to you

Doug

April 30, 2011

A Beautiful day start to
finish

Over all a quiet day for me
one that fit like an old sweater
and an old pair of slippers. the
peepers are at their best this
spring evening I hear them
saying all is well. one of those
days to rejoice and be glad in
The wonder of being caught
up in the creative energy that's
spring, When I was a kid I would
help my mother turn a skein of wool
into balls of potential for her to
work her wonder. Behold I make
all things new Thank you for this
day for the peepers and a recollection

Give us peace this night Lord as we
seek our rest may we praise you
and glorify you forever

With Love

Doug

MAY 1, 2011

Some sun mostly rain a still
day a day the Lord has made
rejoice and be glad.

Each night as I begin I push
a button reading new message
and there it is a blank page days
are like that a new gift *given* to
us to make the most of just as
a blank page is *given* to make
the most of. Do we accept this
gift the gift of a day the Lord has
made? the day is *given* the
acceptance for each of us is
another step in our journey we
move ahead some steps are
hard to take each step is Holy
filling the page step by step
Our Easter story is of *Love* in
action we take each step into
a new day giving the message
of *Love* each step of the way

May the Lord's Peace be upon
you this night may we seek our
rest knowing the Lord is present

With *Love*

Doug

MAY 2, 2011

A chill is back in the air
along with rain and fog

The journey that together
is ours to share never fails
to provide surprises all
journeys are like that it's
the exceptions we need to
be prepared for the routine
will take care of itself. My
journey of faith has been
like that often times I find
myself wandering yet each
of these times has been a
time of discovery renewal
refreshment and new focus
I have come to the conclusion
that we learn and grow from
the exceptions the jogs in the
road that challenge me to look
and see things differently. Lord
for this day I'm thankful keep
me at the task.

Seek rest this night and wake
refreshed for the journey.
Love

Doug

MAY 3, 2011

Rain persisted all day
cool to cold

I want to let you know
that these bits & pieces
will be erratic for the next
little while we will be on the
road seeing gaining a new
perspective learning and
just plain getting caught up
with other companions on
this journey. I will write as
possible.

Find rest tonight be still and
know that the journey goes
on

With Love

Doug

MAY 25, 2011

A beautiful day full of the soft greens
and muted golds and silvers warm

The journey has gone on
these last few days and
nights. Over time I will share
some of the day gems I have
gathered. I have had the good
fortune of being with many
angels boys and girls and a
special girl named Alice she
is a deaf English Setter. We
had just arrived and sat down
when Alice came in ran through
the house and jumped from
about 5feet away landing in my
lap. it was instant stillness the
kind of stillness only angels can
bring. The two of us she in my
lap me with one hand pinned
down translated it all into that
kind of quiet so hard to come
by these days. WoW what a
greeting Alice so close pretending
not to be there Indeed Alice
is an Angel of welcome. Perhaps
like Alice we all need to do more
lap jumping and practice stillness.
tells me that you don't "have to
have it all to do it all"

Seek rest this night with joy

with Love
Doug

May 26, 2011

A warm day almost hot
A spring day almost Summer
Grey sky bright very still
Still could brew a storm

This has been a day rich with
an energy only felt in spring
we are held in a tension birth
promise discovery The white
Ash the late bloomer has set
its buds full of sap and like
clockwork the Orioles are back.
In all this freshness I see the
garments of God laid out
before us ready for the last
fling before the heavy
lifting of summer. Lord be
known to us in the goodness
of creation keep us aware of
the holiness of the ground we
walk on. The air is heavy tonight
as though draped over the trees.
That kind of stillness that promises
a storm There's something up.

May peace be upon each of us this
night. May we be held in the
embrace of the loving Lord. Seek
your rest.

Love
Doug

MAY 27, 2011

A day unsettled that remains
the celestial rumblings and
faint light show persist hope
to get this off

Each day a gift each day
another step in the journey
of renewal and creation each
day is an offering of refreshment
in the restless becoming which
is the journey with the
God of light and Life. Each day
an offering of light and life and
the journey moves on. I'm
thankful for the journey and
each new day. Set us to the
task Lord so we may carry
light and life as we go. Grant
us good humor fill us with joy
keep us young at heart and silly
enough to want to play in the rain
provide us with puddles in the path
to splash. make us thankful as we
go hand in hand with you the
light and life

Let us seek our rest this night and
dream of one day gathering in the
rain with unlimited puddles to splash
Smile Smile Smile we are brothers
and sisters of light and life

Love
Doug

MAY 28, 2011

A day that managed to defy
prediction Even now in the
last slow resolution Maybe

I have often said that spring
is the season we wait for and
often miss thus we look back
with fond recollection. The
journey we are on is not a
matter of searching for God,
it is rather a journey with God.
God of the journey be with us
as we find ways to make you
known may our lives reflect you
may our spirits reflect you may
we carry hope may we bring
light to darkness may we bring
joy may we bring the softness
of your love may we extend a
hand to those who have fallen
may we offer a drink to the thirsty
may we bring humor to show the
richness of your love Keep us at
the little tasks so often forgotten.

May we seek our rest covered
over by the love of God May we
offer ourselves to the little tasks.

With Love

Doug

May 29, 2011

A wonderful start for this
day a Spring day you could
smell and taste a gift indeed
a gift.

The day now hangs heavy
like a pair of jeans on the
clothes line. A day of thank-
fulness for me and others as
well Hugs given and received
Rogation Sunday a day full of
promise and expectation The
Altar covered with flower seed
packets gave the impression
that a rainbow had exploded
leaving behind all it's color to be
blessed and planted with the
hope of a new rainbow the icon
hope.The rainbow always elicits
from me two responses one is
WoW and the other is a quiet
sense of wonder that echos
through those private places
perhaps a tear The author
of Eden still setting his
signature in the heavens.

Let us seek our rest this night
thankful for rainbows. let them
touch you as well the tear its
ok and to think the author of
Eden is in the room with us

Love
Doug

May 30, 2011

The day passing borderline
Summer, a misty start ending
with hot sun still in its ending

Sometimes we miss the wonder
of a new day we get so caught
up in the doing that the being part
is lost. The busyness itself becomes
the focus, it becomes a source of
comfort until we find ourselves
overcome by it all perhaps lost.
There come those times when
the best thing we can do is nothing.
just stop and wait. be still and know.

Rest will come this night in the
quiet of our hearts. be thankful
for the quiet let the stillness be.

Love

Doug

MAY 31, 2011

This day as it closes can
still take credit as Hot maybe
a record.

And so it is we mark and label
and compare and sort. I would
prefer to see each day as the
singular gift that it is to be taken
on its own. for me a day to ponder
picking rhubarb does that for me
a humble plant that requires little
except those elements of the full-
ness of creation. I have a tendency
to want to fuss with the way it is
when just letting them be is best.
This old plant taught me a lesson
about just letting be. I had dug
some for a friend who wanted
some of his own. In the midst of
the digging and separating a
root fell off to the side unnoticed
and unplanted well the root found
that spot suited and it took root
to become the large plant from
which I picked stalks today.

As we seek our rest this night
may we discover those places
where just letting be is wisdom.

Love this night

Doug

JUNE 2, 2011

A day of bright sun perhaps
a sweater? The summer heat
of recent days held back by
the exuberance of Spring.

I find that each day needs to have
some free space. some time
that's open to do magic to lead
in an unexpected direction. a
day more full of surprise than
agenda comes when you leave
the date book at home. I find
going out with my camera
is increasingly a matter of being
found by an image. This journey
we are on will take care of itself
let the surprises in could it be that
all our planning prevents our
becoming? Each day a gift for us
to grasp and keep or to free to grow
and emerge as a gift of beauty.

Let us seek our rest this night in
quiet let us free our days and be free
to discover the newness of life

love

Doug

JUNE 4, 2011

For me a lazy day the day
cool overall warming wink

Things in the country are
graceful this time of year
and a day can just slip by
without notice but not with
my 8 yr. old granddaughter visiting.
"have the little children come to
me." If I had to assemble a
hugging team she would
be my anchor man, she's
the best. There's more to
that quote though. When and
where does one stop being
a child. better still who
decides? If the decision
is not of numbers it must be
of spirit. the spirit of youth
the wonder of newness.
I had an aunt who slept in
the room in which she was born
for 93 yrs. and she always
saw something new out of
those windows. 93 or 8 both
children by the grace of God.

let us each seek our rest this
night with the knowledge that
we are each a child may your
rest be sweet.

with Love
Doug

June 5, 2011

The day passed without
event, Started cool gentle
breeze carried warmth.

This has been a day full of
promise and wonder. John
Dunne poet, cleric (16,17 century)
observed that the profusion of
the ordinary keeps such objects
from being extraordinary. Creation
is marked by what I have always
called outrageous abundance.
Each day is given and we often
miss the rare gift that it is. Keep
us aware Lord of days remind us
often of your hand of abundance
in all things.

seek rest this night hand in hand
with the Lord of creation. may we
know your hand in all things.

Love

Doug

June 6, 2011

The day has come and gone
without much notice warm but
not hot not enough breeze to
kick up anything.

Upon observation it's a day
that had a strength of its own
to become aware of the
substance in the quietness
I know how often I have failed
to realize the statement quiet
makes. We seem to live in a
world dominated by having to
do something no matter what
Yet this day has spoken with
a quiet voice. It's a day drawn
from a stillness a profound mood
A day that has not directed our attention
toward anything or from anything.
Let the quiet be in us that has been
this day.

A day quiet a night of rest in quiet
Let us let the quiet seek us out

Love,
Doug

JUNE 8, 2011

By any standard a Hot
Summer day but June
the 8th? 96 a record?

Be peaceful this day let
it come to you. I find that
I have much better results
with my photography by
being patient be prepared
and be patient. each day in
this journey we are on asks
the same of us be prepared
and be patent. For myself I
have spent time trying to figure
things out. rather than being
open for whatever the tasks
the givenness of a day offers.
Each day is an offering some
obvious some not perhaps a
riddle.

Let's each seek our rest open
to a new day with all that it will
offer. And thankful for the journey

Love
Doug

JUNE 9, 2011

A day that started with the
prospect of another hot
summer day before its time
it mellowed.

My life has been marked by
a condition I call You don't
know from nothin. It goes
like this every time I think I
know what's going on I don't.
Tonight being a case in point It
was to be an ordinary covered
dish at the church. well it wasn't
There was an ordination in June
1963. That began a journey for
these last 48 years bringing me to
St Luke's, Branchport, NY a journey
as full of surprise as this evening
a journey on which I have come to
know God's grace and the capacity
of the church US to love and give
and to hold and to challenge.I started
out with the idea that I was going to
serve this Church US only to discover
that it's the church Yuns that have cared
for me. One can not say thank you and
hope to capture anything of it. let's
be about the journey

Let us seek our rest this night with
confidence peaceful sleep and the
promise of a new day.

Love
Doug

June 10, 2011

Cloudy Sunny off an' on
all day.

Had a chance to go to the
vineyard today and photo-
graph another step in the
goings on in this place
where there's always some-
thing going on. It never
ceases to amaze me how
already they have grown
long canes and set the
flowers as evidence of
abundance of new fruit
My objective today was
to photograph the tiny
promise of a flower. I
must return soon to keep
up with the miracle.

May this night be one of
quiet rest and quiet rest.

Love

Doug

June 12, 2011

After the storm of yesterday
today just could not gather
itself to make its own mark.

It's on these otherwise non-
descript days that miraculous
things so often happen. the
early church had one of those
days and marks it as its birthday.
As though Being touched by the
power of the holy spirit was not
enough something more profound
took place that day. It was a day of
mutual understanding They could
hear and understand one another.
gathered in one place with one accord
listening and hearing. hearing not bad
what a birthday gift.

Seek rest this night listening with
quietness.

Love

Doug

JUNE 13, 2011

A day that to begin with
promised one thing and
produced something else.

Living out a day is like that
Keeping our hearts and
imagination open keeping
our edges smooth and our
assumptions few, so that
we are able to take the
fullness of a day and use
the art of surprise to be
enriched and renewed. The
day is of the Lord's making. It
is for us to gather it up and
be taught. What better teacher
than to sit at the feet of surprise
Keep us open Lord to listen.

May we rest this night and
be surrounded with stillness
through the night.

Love

Doug

June 14, 2011

Today has been one with
a hard edge. A Robust
cold acting like it wants to
stay,

There are days like that days
with hard edges. Edges that
don't yield. There are days that
speak for themselves. These
are the sleepers they take some
working at. These are the days
that can hold rewards if we
work at them. Indeed the days
that push back have in them
the promise of reward, As a
caseworker working with abusive
families I discovered that the
families that pushed back were
the ones that could solve their
problems. It takes edges days
with edges hold the promise of
renewal

Grant this night peace and rest.

Love
Doug

JUNE 16, 2011

It was a mishmash of a day
Going out at any given time
offered a different season.

I have had days like today
full of surprise and variable.
It's been a good day.
This day has brought with it
a sense of peace. It has been
a day that you look back on
and say aha you discover
little gems and you smile
and gather them up and
one at a time you polish
them on your jeans drop
them in a pocket. whistle
(hum?) a little tune and go
about being thankful for all
that the day has become.

Perhaps as we rest this night
(special pillow at the ready)
comforting a shoulder or holding
a knee we will smile say thanks
out loud.

With Love

Doug

June 17, 2011

A late spring day that just
seemed to suit as my mother
would say.

I fall into the trap of thinking
ahead too much. I was just
thinking how many days to
summer. It's the how many
days till. When I start doing
that I tend to miss the little
things and the quietness the
bits and pieces of each day
the little ridges and valleys
that provide the fullness of
a day indeed of life. Living
with a brother who was deaf
taught me how deafness
takes away from a person
the subtlety of speech
removing the texture of life.
If we spent too many days
counting how many days till
this or that the result is living
deafness

seek rest this night feeling the
fullness of being in the present
we will be enriched and Kept safe

Love
Doug

JUNE 18, 2011

The day warmed as it
matured to end hot

This has been a day of
quiet reflection. Taking
what comes neither trying
to figure it out nor move it
in a particular direction.
let the day speak for itself.
That awful urge to do some-
thing wants to overcome
letting the quietness spend
some time with us healing
our hearts and calming our
souls. It's at times like this
that I have awareness of the
Beauty of holiness.

Seek rest this night invite
the beauty of holiness to be
present.

Love

Doug

June 23, 2011

the night rumbled on
with a flash of light here and
there to mark the way. Ending
in Summer

I have days now and then that
just don't seem to fit. no matter
what I do I just feel out of sync
a ramblin' day no apparent focus
or direction. Perhaps days like
this are teacher days or reminder
days. days that say to us who made
you boss. Don't be so full of yourself
as to think you know either the
direction or the pace. Let it be
just take it in stride let be and let love
handle it. Sometimes I have been
going full speed only to discover
I was going in the wrong direction.
let's make sure we're headed in
the right direction before stepping
on the gas. The old railroad crossing
signs had it about right Stop Look
Listen.

Be easy about rest this night it will
come and we will be refreshed

Love,
Doug

JUNE 24, 2011

An ordinary day for us
Black sky west rain with
the trimmings thunder
lightning then sun two
repeat shows.

I tend to want to set the
agenda. It's hard for me
to just go with the flow
And yet I find that letting
go is the way to go. I've
come to the conclusion
that the richest rewards
are found by discovering
the pace and direction that's
there in the givenness
of the day. Go with the
flow dare to be carried

I seek rest this night with
confidence of rest. Find
peace let love in

Love
Doug

June 25, 2011

The air movement was less
than windy and more than
Perhaps a stiff breeze.

A day of movement a day
with a stiff breeze blowing
through it the kind of day
that relies on the season
for its name. Breezes often
come with the change of
seasons. Life can be like
that. It's often acted out
in the choppiness of a breezy
day without any clear time
or place. it's those times between
where much of life is lived.
Gather these days and
celebrate each to its
fullness. Each day a gift
each day a gem to be
polished Days don't so much
need to be understood as
accepted and celebrated.

Find rest as the evening
settles itself over us as a breeze
stirring till the last.

Love,
Doug

About the Author

Doug and his wife Donna live in a self-renovated 1890's farmhouse near Cohocton, NY. They have 4 grown children, 15 grandchildren, and 16 great grandchildren. Doug earned a Master's Degree in Theology and became an ordained Episcopal priest in 1963. At a later time Doug combined a part-time ministry position with a full-time position in Steuben County Child Protective Services.

Doug has many interests, including outdoor activities, woodworking, baking, and photography. He loves people and he is a good listener. He finds himself constantly enriched by the people with whom he is in contact. Laughter is never far from him. His sense of curiosity is like that of a boy turning over stones in a stream.

He is constantly searching for new things. For his 83rd birthday, Doug bought himself a gift of a DJ1 drone, camera included of course. He is often heard saying, "Life is beautiful."

Printed in the United States
By Bookmasters